Thank you to the children who suggested their favourite amazing facts: Tom Bourne-Cox, Lyra Chilton, Rudy Chilton, Calla Mackenzie, Evan Mackenzie — C.B.

Written by Catherine Brereton.
Illustrations by Chris Dickason.
Front cover design by Thy Bui.

Red Shed would also like to thank author Clive Gifford for use of some content from *Fake News* and illustrator Steve James for use of his artwork on pages 12–13.

First published in Great Britain 2021 by Red Shed, part of Farshore
An imprint of HarperCollins*Publishers*
1 London Bridge Street, London SE1 9GF
www.farshore.co.uk

HarperCollins*Publishers*
Macken House, 39/40 Mayor Street Upper,
Dublin 1, D01 C9W8, Ireland

Copyright © HarperCollins*Publishers* Limited 2021

ISBN 978 0 0084 9218 2
Printed and Bound in the UK using 100% Renewable Electricity
at CPI Group (UK) Ltd
006

A CIP catalogue is available from the British Library.

MIX
Paper | Supporting
responsible forestry
FSC™ C007454

This book is produced from independently certified FSC™ paper
to ensure responsible forest management.

For more information visit: www.harpercollins.co.uk/green

AMAZING FACTS

EVERY 7 YEAR OLD

NEEDS TO KNOW

RED SHED

Whether you love animals or adventure, science or sport, you'll find LOADS of weird and wonderful facts ...

What animal wees out of its mouth?

What huge structure is held together with sticky rice?

Which bird can fly backwards?

Where was the world's most expensive banana?

Read on to find out the answers and lots more awesome information ...

A giant squid has eyes as big as your head.

A common shrew needs to eat
something every two or three
hours to survive.

It can eat earthworms that are
bigger than its body.

A crocodile can go for up to three years without eating.

Some sea turtles breathe
through their bottoms and
wee out of their mouths.

A sea turtle can hold its breath
for up to seven hours.

Female sea turtles swim thousands
of kilometres to lay their eggs on the
same beach they hatched on.

In Iceland there is a school where people can learn . . .

A fame school for animals in Germany taught dogs to dance, cats to play the piano and a hen to play the xylophone.

Believe it or not, you have about the same number of hairs on your body as a chimpanzee!

Your body contains enough carbon to make 900 pencils.

On average, people can remember

5,000

faces.

Wombats do cube-shaped poos and leave them to mark where they've been.

Koalas have two thumbs on each front paw.

There is a giant 'Big Koala' statue
in Dadswell's Bridge, Australia.
Australia also has Big Prawn,
Big Guitar and Big Banana statues.

There are millions of pieces of rubbish whizzing around in space.

Space scientists have made a great big net to try and clear up some of the junk.

Rubbish left by astronauts on the Moon includes a hammer, a pair of Moon boots, golf balls and bags of wee.

Astronaut Charles Duke left a family photo on the Moon.

In 2016, Abraham Muñoz from Mexico ran a whole marathon while keeping a football up in the air with his feet and head. He only dropped it four times.

In Lima, Peru, people like to dress up their dogs in the colours of their favourite football team.

Marine iguanas' snot is full of salt – they sneeze it out after drinking salty seawater as they swim.

Hoopoe chicks squirt liquid poo when they are frightened.

It once rained so much in Ipswich, Australia, that sharks swam through the streets.

It hardly ever rains
in Antarctica.

A big storm cloud can weigh as much
as 57 Tyrannosaurus rex dinosaurs!

In the United States, 350 slices of pizza get eaten every second.

More than 500 years ago, some people tried to predict the future by using cheese.

Concorde was the fastest passenger plane ever. It flew at 2,180 kilometres per hour and could travel from London, UK, to New York, United States, in around three hours.

The bullet train in Japan is one of the fastest in the world. It speeds along at over 300 kilometres per hour.

The ancient Romans used wee as a mouthwash to whiten their teeth.

The ancient Romans had a goddess of sewers, called Cloacina, and maybe gods of farts and manure, too.

In the 16th to 17th centuries, there was a craze for drinking crushed-up Egyptian mummies as a health cure.

Ingredients in ancient Egyptian medicine included fly poo, crocodile poo, human poo and 13 other types.

The ancient Egyptians invented toothpaste.

Ancient Egyptian writing is called hieroglyphics and is made up of pictures – a bit like our emojis.

**Male mice sometimes sing
to impress females.**

**A mouse can move its jaw out of
shape to fit through a tiny space.**

A puffin can catch an amazing 60 fish in its beak all at once.

Only female mosquitoes bite. And they don't really bite, but pierce your skin with mouthparts like a sharp straw.

The leaves of a giant water lily found in the Amazon rainforest are so big that they could easily support your weight.

In the Netherlands in the 1600s,
tulips were more valuable than gold.

China used more cement to build things in 2011, 2012 and 2013 than the United States did in the whole of the 20th century.

A school in China built a running track on its roof.

The stones in the Great Wall of China are held together with a mixture containing sticky rice.

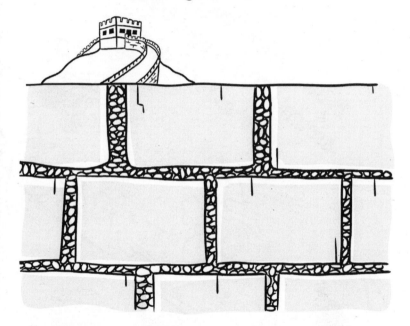

China has more people than any country in the world – more than 1.4 billion people.

In Switzerland every January, around 1,500 people dress up as witches for a ski race.

One mountain in Switzerland has a staircase all the way up – with 11,674 steps!

A sloth sticks out its very long tongue to get its food so it doesn't have to move to eat.

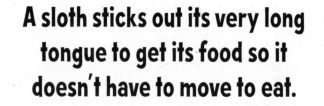

The word 'sloth' means 'lazy', and sloths usually move less than 40 metres a day. That's about the length of three London buses.

A sloth only climbs down from the trees once a week to go to the toilet.

There was a prehistoric sloth
as tall as two elephants.

A cow drinks enough water every day to fill a bathtub.

Herds of thirsty zebras travel up to 1,000 kilometres every year to find the juiciest grass. That's nearly the distance from London to Edinburgh and back.

A group of zebras is called a dazzle.

Flamingos get their pink colour from the algae, larvae and pink shrimps they eat.

Butterflies, pigeons and goldfish can all see more colours than we can.

Chameleons can change colour when they're angry or stressed.

The Arctic fox changes colour from grey-brown to white in winter so it can hide in the snow.

In Saint Paul, Canada, there is a huge landing pad built to welcome any aliens that might land one day.

In the 16th century, the Groom of the Stool's job was to look after King Henry VIII's personal toilet and even wipe his bottom!

Today, vomit collectors have
a gross job. They clean up sick
underneath scary rollercoasters.

Tyrannosaurus rex had a mouth so big
it could have swallowed you whole.

Each one of its teeth was up to
20 centimetres long – about
as long as the top part
of your arm.

The duckbill dinosaur Parasaurolophus (say 'pa-ra-saw-roll-o-fus') had a crest on its head that it probably used like a trumpet.

Potatoes have been grown by astronauts in space.

Broccoli is actually a flower.

In the 1830s, tomato ketchup was sold as medicine to cure indigestion and diarrhoea.

Olympus Mons, the tallest mountain in the Solar System, is on the planet Mars.

There are lots of space robots on Mars, exploring its surface.

In 1938, a radio play about Martians invading Earth caused panic. People thought it was really happening.

Sudha Cars Museum in India has cars shaped like footballs, aubergines, burgers and handbags.

**Cars 'kick' a giant football in
the German game of autoball.**

Slugs and snails have around 27,000 teeth.

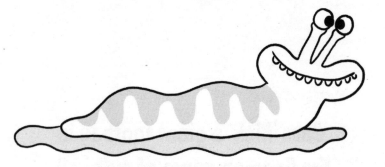

In winter, a lid of dried slime over the entrance to its shell keeps a snail snug while it hibernates.

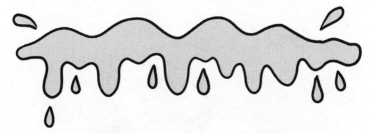

Long ago, people would rub a snail on a burn to heal it.

Scientists are busy making slug and snail slime into a stretchy glue to mend people's cuts.

Parrots can learn to copy human words – a blue parakeet called Puck once learned 1,728 words!

Parrots can even learn to copy people singing.

Grasshoppers sing by rubbing their back legs against their front wings like a violin.

Most birds sing or call using their beaks and throat, but a rainforest bird called the manakin plays music on its wings.

More than 50 different types of dinosaur have been found in one area of Alberta, Canada. No wonder it's called Dinosaur Provincial Park.

Fourteen dinosaur nests full of hatched and unhatched eggs have been found in the United States in an area called . . . Egg Mountain.

Your brain stays busy even when you are asleep.

Your brain is the greediest part of your body – it uses one-fifth of all your energy.

Octopuses are good at brain games such as solving puzzles and mazes.

The kangaroo rat can jump more than
2 metres high with its long back legs.
It hops around in the desert.

The person who invented the trampoline showed it off by jumping on it with a kangaroo.

Horses can sleep both lying down and standing up.

Horses can only breathe through their noses, not their mouths.

In 2002, runner Tom Johnson raced against a horse in an 80-kilometre race. The man won by 10 seconds!

The city of Bergen, Norway, has an elaborate gingerbread city every Christmastime.

The biggest gingerbread house ever
was built in Texas, United States.
It was taller than a Christmas tree
and used 7,200 eggs!

There are more pet tigers and zoo tigers in the United States than wild tigers in the whole world.

A tiger is one of the highest-jumping animals – it can spring 4 metres high.

A tiny flea can jump 200 times its own body length.

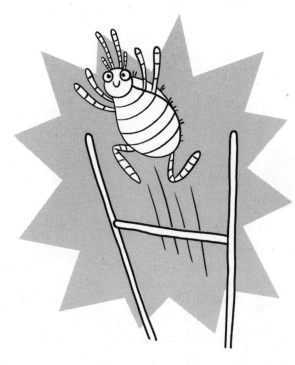

That's a bit like you jumping twice as high as the London Eye.

An ordinary banana taped to the wall was put on display in an American art gallery in 2019. It then sold for $120,000!

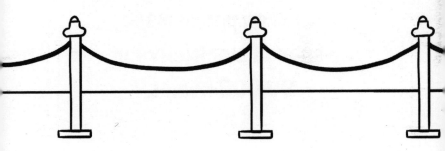

A power plant in the
Netherlands uses
chicken poo to make
enough electricity for
90,000 homes.

A Kenyan man called Anthony Mutua invented shoes that produce enough electricity to charge a mobile phone.

**Your funny bone is not a bone
at all – it is a nerve in your elbow
that tingles when you knock it.**

**More than half of your bones
are in your hands and feet.**

Sharks don't have bones,
but their skeleton is made
of a rubbery, gristly material
called cartilage – like you
have in your nose.

In the 17th and 18th centuries, garden gnomes used to be real people hired to decorate a rich person's garden.

Shane Wilmott built a mini skate park in his Australian garden . . . for his pet mice.

It is illegal to build sandcastles on one beach near Venice, Italy.

A type of fruit called the durian is so stinky that it's against the law to take one on a bus in Singapore.

A law in the Philippines says students can't finish secondary school until they have planted ten trees.

Blackbirds, nightingales, ferrets and monkeys were popular pets in ancient Rome.

The Circus Maximus, where Romans watched chariot races, was bigger than any sports stadium today.

**Monkeys have tails,
while apes do not.**

**Monkeys can understand
written numbers and can even
count and do sums.**

Some monkeys in Japan share food
with deer and hitch a ride
on their backs.

The world's smallest monkey,
the pygmy marmoset, is only
as big as a hamster.

**Bats are the only mammals
that can fly.**

A bat can catch thousands of insects to eat every night.

Without bats, we wouldn't have avocados, mangoes or bananas. The bats spread pollen, which helps these plants grow new seeds.

Bats groom themselves like cats do.

A snake milker's job is to collect venom from snakes to use in medicines. Yikes!

A dog food tester's job is to
taste . . . you guessed it, dog food!
Just to check it's good enough
for our doggy friends.

Red handfish use their fins to 'walk' across the bottom of the sea instead of swimming.

Owls can't move their eyeballs.

Hummingbirds can fly backwards.

In 2011, in a winners' parade, footballer Sergio Ramos of Real Madrid dropped the trophy and it was run over.

The original football World Cup trophy was stolen from an exhibition in London in 1966. A dog called Pickles found it and became a celebrity.

One factory can wrap 64,800 chocolate bars in an hour!

Ruth Wakefield invented the chocolate chip cookie and then sold the recipe in exchange for a lifetime's supply of chocolate.